Grow Up

Three Perspectives to Responsibility

Precious Eda

ISBN 978-93-5610-400-6

Published in India 2022 by Pencil

A brand of
One Point Six Technologies Pvt. Ltd.
123, Building J2, Shram Seva Premises,
Wadala Truck Terminal, Wadala (E)
Mumbai 400037, Maharashtra, INDIA
E connect@thepencilapp.com
W www.thepencilapp.com

DISCLAIMER: *The opinions expressed in this book are those of the authors and do not purport to reflect the views of the Publisher.*

Author biography

*** Precious Eda is a leader with a passion for seeing people become better than they already are. He believes in and pursues his life-purpose which is to add value to everyone he meets.

With over 15 years spent in leading people at various levels, he lives with a commitment towards growing more leaders through teaching leadership and personal development.

He is a Speaker, Teacher, Mentor to many and a trained Attorney.

*** His Series of mini-books treat singular issues in the very vast subject of leadership in each of its series.

It is designed to make key issues and principles in leadership easy to understand and apply to everyday situations.

***. This work – Grow Up, is part of a series of mini-books that treat single points in the very vast topic of leadership in each of its publications.

*** Other books in the series include:

Precious Eda on – Vision, Values, Teamwork…

*** Precious Eda is blessed to share his life with Amarachi Loveth his amazing wife.

CONTENTS

Foreword

One of the major problems plaguing the people of this generation is the attitude of lack of personal responsibility. We all complain and show concern for the breakdown of nearly every institution in our system as a nation and who's fault? We always refer to those who were before us. This may be correct somehow, but it becomes a problem when we go on blaming others for our own short-comings. This is the height of irresponsibility.

As a Nigerian, the lofty examples of irresponsibility just abound all around. For instance, the present administration in power led by President Muhammadu Buhari spent virtually the entire of his first four years in office blaming the previous president for the woeful situation of the country and even for his own inabilities to lead effectively. I still think it is a miracle he was able to win a second term. Well, I live in Nigeria, and miracles happen always. In some ways, we are like God with whom nothing is impossible.

I can say from experience, that the most frustrating people to work with are people who never take responsibility. The worst of the bulk are those who only work to avoid taking responsibility.

Taking responsibility is a duty that only the brave can handle. The idea is in looking inwards first before pointing the finger outside. Not many leaders can dare walk the responsibility road. In fact, leadership offers great excuses for not taking responsibility (at least as shown by many leaders). Having worked under many leaders and held quite a number of positions in various leadership settings, I can tell first hand that the most acceptable attitude of leaders in times of challenges is to duck from responsibility. Take a look at politics today, all over the world, leaders are so quick to blame others and other circumstances in the face of challenges. Leaders find it difficult to boldly tell publicly their true justifications for their actions. And that's why we currently have a dart of excellent leaders in the world today.

I have always thought of the next generation, and the kind of legacy that would be left for the leaders of the future. How would the leaders that look up to us today define the values that we portray and how will they live in their leadership tomorrow?

That's the key question I try to look at in this book. Though not directly, but the perspectives from which I analyse the issue of responsibility mirrors my heart for the leaders of this generation, and more importantly the next generation.

What is Responsibility?

I'd like to look at responsibility from three main perspectives. These three perspectives reflect the meaning of responsibility universally.

Firstly, responsibility implies the duty to deal with or take care of something or somebody.

Secondly, it means taking the blame for something gone wrong.

Thirdly, responsibility is the duty to do something.

So, let's dive-in straight away and consider the issue of Responsibility in the light of the three perspectives...

Acknowledgements

To my Mum,

Dorathy...

You taught me to be responsible

Chapter One... The 1st Perspective

"Responsibility implies the duty to deal with or take care of something or somebody."

In the first instance, it should be realised that at a certain age, we become at least 80 percent responsible for the outcome of our lives. Once you reach the age of social accountability, once you begin to exhibit traits of the need for self-reliance, it simply shows that you have come to the age of responsibility. But the painful truth is that many people want independence so quickly but do not want to take responsibility for themselves that quickly. We must start making choices for ourselves. Begin to show your sense of responsibility to the people over you and then you'll have the measure of freedom you desire. Many people get into fights with their parents or guidance, bosses, stewards and those sort persons over issues of choices and freedom. But sadly, these people more often than not depend almost totally on the help and care of the people they desire independence from. If you do not show people how responsible you've become, they'll never trust you enough to treat you like a responsible person.

Grow up! Quit kidding around! Show how much you can take care of yourself. You cannot continue to rely on someone else for everything and expect to be in total control of your life. I am certainly not encouraging rebellion, but the truth is, we must not hide behind seeming deprivation to become nuisance to society. How long would you continue to blame others for who you have become or what happens to you? The quality of the life you live is a reflection of the quality of choices you make. You make good rich choices, you become good and rich. You make bad poor choices and you become bad and poor. To take responsibility for your life means to personally dictate your daily outcomes and being influenced by forces you personally choose and not those chosen for you.

Take a look around you and ask yourself; who are the people I look up to? What are the things that influence me? What are the places I like being at? Who are the people I like being around? When you answer these questions, then ask yourself; did I choose them or did they choose me? Did I find them or did they find me? When you're done honestly answering that, go ahead to ask; what is the quality of my life right now?

I tell you, if your life's quality is not appealing to you, then you should start a rethink on those questions. Many of us fail to take responsibility for ourselves because we have no standards for our lives.

If you don't set a standard for your life, you will live by the standards of other people.

What are your moral standards? Do you do things simply because people you know do them? Do you go to places just because your friends go there? Are your actions directly influenced by your calculated decisions? You must take responsibility and take care of you for you.

It's good to look up to others, but do the ones you look up to realistically reflect a similarity to your genuine personality? Think and discover who you really are. Seek God and find your purpose and then choose your influences in line with where you want to go and who you want to become.

Wherever you find yourself today, in school, at work, wherever, take responsibility today. Quit complaining of being used, being messed up, being deprived or being left behind. Get up and decide to be different by choosing who you get to be with, where you want to be at and how you want to be.

It was Sigmund Freud who said ***"Most people do not really want freedom, because freedom involves responsibility, and most people are frightened of responsibility".***

If, you want to see a change in your life, stand up and face your challenges for yourself because if you don't, no one will face them for you.

You are where you are because you chose to be where you are. Quit day-dreaming and living in the fantasy that everything will fall into place somehow for you and you'll become your dream.

Do not be deceived, nothing would ever move if a force is not applied to it. Be the one to apply the force for you and make things happen for yourself. Don't think help will fall from the skies for you. The truth is an external help can only come at the point when you can no longer help yourself. Have you tried all you can to totally help yourself? For many the answer is not yet, so no one will help you.

It's amazing how we dream so big and imagine mind blowing imaginations everyday yet we sit at a place and do nothing about the dreams and imaginations. A dream will always remain a dream no matter how real it appears to be. Be responsible! Take the first step! Nobody can pursue your dream better than you can.

Success is a daily achievement of set goals and targets. It means no matter how good your plans are, if you do nothing about them every day, you are failing.

I always tell young people; you can't afford to sleep many hours a day and expect to end up a success. The constant need for relaxation by a young person is the sign of immaturity and irresponsibility. Why do you always need to rest? If the number of hours you put in to work every day as a youth is far less than the number of hours you put in to sleep, there is a sign of laxity or laziness somewhere.

If the size of your dream is far bigger than the chunk of energy you exert to achieving it, then you just may not be doing enough to bring it to reality.

The greatest resources available to a young person are time, money and energy. How and where do you spend your time? Everybody is allotted the same 24 hours every day, but not everybody makes good use of them for profitability. What you spend your time doing is what you end up becoming. You can never achieve all your dreams if you spend all your free time in less productive agendas. Too much movies, too much chatting, too much visiting, too much messing around will all lead to too less achievements.

How, where, on what and on whom do you spend your money? It's crazy to know that most of the drunkards in town are young people. Most of the gamblers around are young people.

You must know that the way you spend your youth will affect the way spend your old age if at all you would live to grow old. Many diseases suffered by many old people are a direct consequence of their youthful escapades. When you spend the little money you have and get on always having fun, one day you will grow old, and you'll no longer be able to have fun because you won't find most things funny anymore. I'm not saying it is wrong to have a good time once in a while, but do you really have that fun once in a while or always at every chance?

We all want to become millionaires and billionaires, but we must understand that we cannot afford to be riotous in spending and end up wealthy. No rich man who got wealthy through hard work and creativity can afford to always be in the club or in joints enjoying life, they are always too busy trying to keep the money they've earned and earn more.

The Bible encourages young people to have a good time in Ecclesiastes 7, but it was quick to advise us to remember our creator too because the days would surely come when all the pleasures we took from our youth will either be regretted or will give us no chance to even look back upon life.

Youths stand out because of the amount of energy they possess. Every sport in the world today is dominated by youths because we are the ones with the energy to compete. It's so disheartening to see young people sit idle all day, sleep all afternoon and then complain of no money. It's a shame to know that we have enough energy to pull down a sky scraper resident in us, yet we leave it unused and untapped.

When last did you work so hard that you had to give up because you could no longer give any more energy to the work? We always want to run away or give excuses when we face hard work, many young people run away from home, quit their little jobs just because they feel the work they are being asked to is too hard, but the truth must be told, hard work doesn't kill, it's foolish work that does. Some young people have gotten into fights with their parents, guardians, older siblings, bosses and others just because they are given hard tasks to accomplish. This is irresponsibility; it shows you cannot care for yourself.

You can never be deliberately placed in charge of others if you cannot be in charge of yourself. If some how you are placed to lead others when you cannot lead yourself, you'll end up taking orders from those you are supposed to be ordering, and this is poor leadership. When you cannot be the captain of your own boat, you should never be made a captain in the first place. Channel your energy towards positive productive activities. Don't sit back at home wasting all your energy on sleep which semi death. Don't turn your office to a relaxation joint where all you do with your free time is watch soaps and series, or play games and watch movies, or chat and gossip. This is wrong energy application, and most times the product is negative productivity. Get up and do some work, it won't kill you. Put your hands and feet to work, don't fold them or cross them and sit back.

I heard a story in the movie courageous; it said that God promised to send rain for two farmers after many years of drought. One farmer in joy over the promise went home and called all his friends to celebrate and be merry with him. The other farmer went home and gathered his tools and workers and went straight into the fields to start planting. The question was then asked, among the two farmers, which one would enjoy the rain? Of course, I don't need to tell you the answer. Yes, they say he who laughs last laughs best, but I must tell you this, a good end will only come to those who plan for it.

Be responsible for your dreams. Take care of yourself and deal with your issues by yourself today. Be responsible. Take responsibility.

Chapter Two... 2nd Perspective

"Responsibility means taking the blame for something gone wrong"

When I think about this perspective of responsibility, football always comes to my mind. In modern day soccer, there is this huge investment people make into the game that drives their interests. So, you find that most times when a team fails or consistently gets poor results, the coach is fired. In fact, there is this popular saying that in football there are only two kinds of coaches: the ones that have been fired and the ones waiting to be fired.

Although I'm not a big fan of firing and hiring coaches just because the team lost a string of games, but this attitude reminds me of the responsibility aspect of leadership and the fact that when something goes wrong someone has to take the blame.

You see, we have a very bad culture of always blaming someone else whenever we fail in one aspect of our lives or the other. When students fail exams, the lecturer was wicked, when an employee gets fired the boss is wicked, when there is lawlessness in town the government is not working. It is always someone else' fault that something bad has happened to us. The truth is, one of the reasons why fingers were created was so they could be used for pointing.

There will always be someone to point at with your finger of accusation. The height of this blame game is when people in their right minds and right senses do wrongs or commit crimes and when they are caught, they blame the devil for making them commit the crimes.

It only shows the level of irresponsibility we have as a people. I know that there are devils at work who try to destroy, to steal and to kill, but we must understand that it's he who breaks the hedge that the serpent will bite. So somehow, the devil has to use an available agent. It's such a shame to notice how this attitude of pointing fingers has overtaken this generation and the young people in it. You see young people with active and creative minds and with lots of energy within them sit at home and do nothing whiling away precious time, wishing and day dreaming of big success, and when it doesn't happen or when it's too late to do something about so many things gone wrong in their lives, they turn around to blame someone else; the father who did not send them to school, the uncle who did not pay their school fees, the government that did not provide a job for them or better still, the witch that witch-hunted their progress.

The most important power available to any human being alive is the power of choice. We all have the power to choose who and what we will become and where we will end up. There are people in this world that had all the odds against them yet they turned out as great imparters of humanity, many had disabilities that were serious enough to discourage them, yet they did not consider their shortcomings. Some had the opportunity to fail and blame someone else, yet they chose to take responsibility and fight for their lives.

If Nelson Mandela had blamed the government for discriminatory policies and sat at home to do nothing about it, South Africa would not be free, but he took responsibility knowing that the ever-present judging-judge (his conscience) would never let him rest in peace if he did nothing about apartheid. Today he is dead and gone yet people still hold symposiums to remember his contributions to humanity.

If Martin Luther King Jr. had decided to blame the government for being wicked or even blame Africans for selling their brothers as slaves, it would have been the perfect excuse for him not to be mentioned in American history as a leader. Dr King could have done nothing and decided to continue suffering and attract pity from the rest of the world. But no! He took responsibility. He decided to take the blame if change refused to happen. He went as far as paying the ultimate price for what he believed in. American history will be incomplete without mentioning the contributions of Dr King.

Ben Carson was told he had no brains. They said he was the dumbest dummy in his class. Enough reasons to throw in the towel and point to someone for his condition. But resiliently, Ben Carson worked hard, studied hard, prayed hard and became one of the best surgeons to ever grace the field of medicine in the world.

Who do you blame when things go wrong? When something bad happens, do you rush to point the finger, or do you first ask yourself, where did I fail? We need to change our blaming attitude if we want our lives and our societies to go forward.

For me in Nigeria, I think it is a shame to us all when people in authority or government are corrupt because we are the government. The man at the top has a home, a community, a town, a family. Bad will produce bad. Corruption will produce corruption. Whether we like it or not, one way or another, we all have benefited from corruption even if it is the tiniest practice. The extra money you make at the office that is not properly accounted for, the extra tips you get for showing illegal favours. The undue preferential treatments you get at the expense of others because of your large pocket. Those extra scores we get in examinations that are induced by cash or kind favours. One way or another, we have all benefited from corruption.

It is surprising to still see people point fingers at others and call others wicked when their stories come out in the press when in fact, we are the more wicked ones.

If we stop the little bad, it will not grow to become the mighty evil. We must learn to take the blame first when things go wrong. We must stop and change. We have no right to blame our leaders if we too are guilty.

Truly, sometimes things happen and we are totally not to be blamed. When it is not your fault, yes, it's understandable. But even then, don't sit down with the problem and waste your time analysing whose fault it is or is not. Make personal efforts to find solutions.

One mistake many people make is always dwelling in the past. When they had made mistakes with their lives before, they always make reference to those errors and such references will always draw you back and hinder you from focusing on your all-important future.

Now you did well by taking responsibility for your actions, but the purpose of taking responsibility is not to let your faults serve as handcuffs or prison cells over your life. They should serve as teachers and pointers to a new direction, away from similar failures. Every mistake is a stepping stone. When you know that you have failed, it means you should know that you can succeed. Do not remain in the failures of the past. A wise man once said "if you stay with your past, you will pass with your past". Now that's true. No one ever looks backwards while walking forward. You have done well to take responsibility for your actions; it's time to draw inspiration from the experience you have gotten. Your ability to learn from your own faults and make progress is one of the highest senses of responsibility you can have for yourself.

No matter how close people are to you, they can never experience exactly the same thing you experience all the time. You are the one in the best position to decide for yourself if you want to go forward or remain behind. Take responsibility today, not just for the wrongs you've done but also for the rights you can do.

Many times, when things happen, they may never be our faults, but we all are leaders of ourselves and others and one of the hallmarks of an effective leader is the ability to assume responsibility.

A good leader will seek a solution before thinking of an excuse. Your ability to show the way forward when everyone is asking why something wrong had to happen is a mark of progressive leadership because in showing the way forward you will definitely come across the whys. If we must change as a people, we must develop the solution attitude and not remain with the situation attitude.

The situation attitude looks at the problem and remains with it always trying to mourn and groan and blame.

But the solution attitude sees the problems, with a solution in mind, finds out the reason for the problem, thinks of the way out and provides one. If every one of us can develop this attitude consciously within us, we will continually experience a change in our lives. We cannot afford to live irresponsible lives by always dodging the truth. We must face the truth and allow it to build our lives.

Take responsibility for your actions, for your failures, for your successes and for people under you. Know that it will always fall on you to do the right thing always and if you don't act, no other person can act for you.

Chapter Three... 3rd Perspective

"Responsibility is the duty to do something"

I have wondered why people hardly share things like money, gifts and material things. When it comes to profitable issues or matters in which people tend to directly benefit personally from, they become greedy. But no one is ever greedy with taking responsibility.

I remember the remarkable story of Adam and Eve who after eating the forbidden fruit decided to act a play titled "it wasn't me". At the end of the day, they were still punished for a wrong that wasn't their faults.

You see, that's what many of us do and that's why our society is where it is today. The streets are dirty and it's not my fault, there is no electricity and it's not my fault, people are dying and it's not my fault. But do you know that for every problem you identify, there is something you can do about it? If only we could take responsibility and do something about all the wrongs we see, we will see change.

How many times have people cheated or broken the law in your presence and you did nothing about it? How many times have lies been told before you and you could not even say a word? Many times, we fail to act in such situations, not because of fear but because we just somehow feel that that's the way it has been and so that's the way it is. If we desire to see change, we must always do something.

We complain of poverty in our land and how the government is not living up to expectations, but in our own little ways, how many times have you given something to a poor person or helped someone in need?

When I decided to start my podcast and YouTube channel, it was because I was tired of just sitting back and complaining of all the things that have gone wrong with people and the society. I thought that by putting my voice on the radar, I would be heard, and the solutions I proffer could be taken by someone somewhere. This was also the main thinking behind my starting a blog. And then when it came to writing books on leadership and personal development, I had identified a need in mentorship and a gap in information sharing especially with young leaders. I thought I had a great deal of experience with leadership at many levels so if I could simplify many of the lofty principles of leadership and share personal experiences, perhaps I would be able to reach many more leaders in an effective manner.

So it was for me, having identified the problems, I wouldn't just sit back and bemoan the failures of the system and the people. I have to make a contribution. I have a sense of duty to humanity to proffer solutions to problems I see. My Pastor, Tari Hudson Ekiyor always says that whenever you identify a problem, chances are that you have the solution.

Leadership must be solution driven. Many leaders are problem creators, not solution providers.

As I write this book, President Vladimir Putin has ordered Russian troops to invade Ukraine. His reason? To restore order, and drive out pro-Nazi extremists. I'm quite sure even you reading this paragraph would find this reason laughable. But that's his reason and he is ready to cause untold bloodshed not just in Ukraine, but in Europe and any part of the world that stands in his way. And this is the 21st century, you can imagine that people, I mean organised human being in their right minds shouldn't be thinking of war as an option to conflict resolution. But the Russian leader in providing his solution to a problem only he has identified has now created more problems with tensions rising all over the world. There is now the fear of a World War III.

Leadership must show the attitude of solutions providers. People look up to leaders. People look up to people. And if people or leaders can effectively provide solutions, leadership is successful and influence is multiplied.

We must awaken our instincts to taking responsibility. Don't wait for someone else to step up for you. When you find a challenge and you know what to do to make things right, take up the responsibility and do it. If you have the ability to do whatever it takes for things to work rightly, then go ahead. If the ability or capacity is lacking, then find someone who has ability and capacity to make things right, but don't sit idly by and hope that other people would see what you have seen and do nothing about it.

Quotes on taking Responsibility...

In order to win and succeed in life, responsibility is so important. This is a part of being an adult and learning how to be responsible for everything –

Tonya R. Owens, How to Win and Succeed in Life

Freedom without responsibility is like weight without gravity in physics — a logical impossibility –

Robert C. Solomon, It's Good Business

If you can take responsibility for your own life, then you will begin to realize that you can change it –

H. K. Abell, Being Human

No matter who betrays or rejects you, only you can take responsibility for your mental attitude –

John Hagee, God's Two-Minute Warning

Responsibility is demonstrated by actions and deeds; not by words or information inserted in some glossy magazines or corporate websites. –

Samuel O Idowu, Walter Leal Filho, ʹProfessionals Perspectives of Corporate Social Responsibility

Start to reflect on your life after you accept, act, and take responsibility for your life. –

C. Payne, Attitude Within the Workplace

By choosing to take responsibility for your life, you will immediately gain an increased power to achieve your greatest potential. –

Skip Downing, On Course

Each one of us is responsible for the world - each one of us must give a hand to build our world in a humane manner, crossing faith, fate and family. –

Abhijit Naskar, Operation Justice

Take responsibility for yourself; it's very rewarding. -

Amanda Green, Living with depression and anxiety

The game is my life. It demands loyalty and responsibility, and it gives me back fulfillment and peace. –

Michael Jordan

We have a responsibility to influence the people in our lives to be the best possible people they can be: "Therefore encourage one another and build each other up" (1 Thess. 5: 11). –

Henry Cloud, John Townsend; How to Have That Difficult Conversation

Deliberately take the responsibility to change your life because you can; yes you can! –

Okorote Emmanuel, Don't Take Care; Take The Chance!

Accept responsibility for your life. Know that it is you who will get you where you want to go, no one else. –

Les Brown

Notes

Other books by the author...
VISION
THE CORE
TOP SQUAD
PRECIOUS EDA
To place an order for e-copies or hardcopies of these works...
Call today! - +2347086668850
Or reach Precious on Facebook @iPreciousEda
Or visit preciouseda.blogspot.com
Precious Eda
#1 Millennial in Leadership

Precious
Eda
#iLEADERSHIP

www.ingramcontent.com/pod-product-compliance
Lightning Source LLC
LaVergne TN
LVHW050429160726
843469LV00041B/1287

* 9 7 8 9 3 5 6 1 0 4 0 0 6 *